MW01025622

Pure Love

Jason Evert

Totus Tuus
PRESS
2018

Pure Love
Jason Evert
© 2018 Totus Tuus Press, LLC.
Seventh Edition

Published by Totus Tuus Press, LLC.
P.O. Box 5065
Scottsdale, AZ, 85261
www.totustuuspress.com

Cover by Devin Schadt
Interior by Russell Graphic Design

Printed in the United States of America

978-0-9830923-9-1
978-1-944578-93-0 eBook

If you're like me, you've been told that sex is bad. But when you ask why, you hear something like, "It's just bad, so don't do it," or "You'll get a disease or get pregnant!" While I'm sure you realize that sex has its consequences—and they might be bad if they happen—these reasons aren't always convincing.

Our generation has been taught how to avoid venereal infections, but what we really want to know is how to find, build, and maintain a relationship of real love. Sex is supposed to be a great gift, so it's easy to get tired of hearing about the diseases and unwed pregnancy rates. If you're ready for a different approach, and you want the gift of sex to be as great as it was meant to be, read on.

"How do I find love?"

Everyone wants love. Everyone longs to give himself or herself to another. We're made for love, and that need in us is so deep that many would rather risk getting pregnant or getting an STD than live without love. We may be willing to take these risks because the world tells us that sex equals love. Then we see relationships in which sex destroyed love, and we wonder what went wrong. The only solution capable of breaking through this hurt and confusion is the virtue known as chastity.

"What's chastity?"

Chastity is a virtue (like courage or honesty) that

applies to a person's sexuality. It means that you order your sexual desires according to the demands of real love. For example, when you love a person, you do whatever is necessary to keep from harming them, and you're willing to make heroic sacrifices in order to do what is best for them. Chastity means that you take this definition of love and apply it to sex.

Some think that chastity simply means "no sex." But that's abstinence: focusing on what you can't do and can't have. Chastity focuses on what you can do and can have, right now: a lifestyle that brings freedom, respect, peace, and even romance—without regret.

Because chastity involves purity and self-control, some people think it means sexual repression. On the contrary, it frees a couple from the selfish attitude of using each other as objects, thus making them capable of true love.

"How do you know when it's love?"

You can never judge the value of a relationship by the intensity of the feelings, because these will always come and go. Feeling in love is exciting, but emotions should never be confused with love. For example, a young man might have genuine feelings for a girl, but this does not guarantee that he loves her. The real measure of love is doing what's best for the beloved. Sure, this is demanding. That's why true love is so rare, and that's what makes it so beautiful and worth it.

The opposite of loving is using. For example, guys often use girls for physical gratification, and girls may use guys for social or emotional gratification. But they're never satisfied. I've spoken to more than a million high school and college students, and I've never met a girl who longed for a series of physical relationships. But I've met countless discouraged young women who were trying to find love by doing just this. Maybe they were confusing physical affection with love, or were looking for some affirmation of their worth that their dads never gave them. Either way, these girls weren't finding what they wanted.

Likewise, I've met "players" who said they longed to know how to love women instead of destroying them. They didn't intend to harm girls, but no one ever showed them—or expected them—to treat women with reverence. Dissatisfied with the lifestyle of "getting some," they realized that to conquer a woman sexually was to miss the point of being a man. Only with the fullest giving of themselves in authentic love will they ever find themselves.

If you're sexually active and trying to figure out if it's love, apply the love test. Take the sexual part out of the relationship and live the virtue of chastity. When you remove the lust, you can see if there was ever any love to begin with. Don't be afraid to do this, because *only when love is put to the test can its real value be seen.*[1]

"What if we really love each other?"

If you really love each other, then you'll do what's best for your relationship. However, eighty percent of the time, the physical intimacy of a teen's first sexual relationship won't last more than six months.[2] A couple might think that the statistics won't apply to them because they care so much about each other. But if a guy is sleeping with a woman who is not his wife, is he really doing what is best for her? If he is, then why would he jump out her bedroom window if he heard her dad's footsteps coming down the hall? It's because he knows that their mutual feelings of admiration and attraction do not make their sexual activity an act of love.

Once sex enters the picture, it often becomes the relationship's center, forcing everything else aside. Both people become objects to be used instead of persons to be loved, even though they may not intend this, and will rarely admit to seeing each other that way. One college student said, "I thought sex was going to make us so much closer as a couple. But before long, he didn't want to spend time with *me* any more—he wanted to spend time with *my body*. Looking back, I now realize that I wasn't in love with *him*. I was in love with the feeling of being wanted by someone."

Your body is a gift, and during the sexual act, the couple give themselves to each other. But to reduce this gift to a loan gives you less respect than you deserve. That's why the total gift of one's body and heart belongs in a permanent and faithful relationship: marriage. We might feel like we're more "in love" than some married people, but emotions don't create a marriage, and they can't hold one together.

Also, you can't truly give yourself unless you realize your worth and the magnitude of the gift you're exchanging. True love says, "You are everything to me. I give myself totally to you forever." This is the real commitment that springs from the heart of every person who is sincerely in love. It demands permanence, not just hooking up. It does not insist on its own way when desires are strong, and it can sacrifice the desires of the moment for something permanent. After all, if you can't say "no" to sex, then what is your "yes" worth?

"How can it be wrong if no one gets hurt?"

Although it may be hard to see now, sex outside of marriage hurts both people. Besides the obvious risks of disease and unwanted pregnancy, it scars them emotionally. One husband admitted, "I would do anything—*anything*—to forget the sexual experiences I had before I met my wife. . . . The pictures of the other women from my past go through my head, and it's killing any intimacy. The truth is that I've been married to this wonderful woman for eight years and I have never

9

been 'alone' in the bedroom with her."[3] If and when you get married, the sexual experiences you've had with others may weigh upon the heart of your future spouse, not to mention the spouse of the person you're dating. This obviously isn't good for any marriage.

Even if a couple doesn't think that anyone is getting hurt, they may be using sex to cover up problems, which only makes things worse. When this happens, one gynecologist said, "Many teenagers feel that something is wrong—not with sex itself, but with themselves. So they try harder to make sex 'work,' to make sex provide those things they think it should: intimacy, love, trust, acceptance, appreciation of their masculinity or femininity, relief from their loneliness. When it doesn't work, millions of teenagers . . . turn their anger and hurt inward, resulting in depression. . . . We repeatedly return to certain behaviors such as sex, drugs, or drinking to get something that continually eludes us."[4]

Sex outside of marriage also usually hurts our relationship with our parents because that lifestyle is often accompanied by lies. Gossip often follows at school, and otherwise lasting friendships are sometimes sacrificed for a date who doesn't last. One high school girl emailed me, saying, "I have lost friends, but most of all I have lost myself. I feel as if I am unlovable; therefore the only type of love I can receive is fake sexual love. Anyone around me would think I'm just a happy normal teenager, but if everything were so good, I wouldn't be crying at night."

Deeper than all of this is the spiritual harm, because sin separates us from God. With sins of lust, the pleasure gained is nothing when compared to what we lose. So a better question to ask is this: Who *isn't* hurt by premarital sex? This may be difficult to understand right now, because it's tough to see beyond the circle of your friends and the walls of your school. But it's wise to not make any life-changing decisions based on the opinions of classmates, most of whom you'll never see again after graduation.

"What if we're both okay with it?"

Ever hear a girl say the following? "I'm seeing this guy my friends and family hate. They say he's possessive, but that's the way he shows how much he cares. I started having sex with him because I really care about him, too. Why can't people see how great he is?"

Although this girl thinks the problem is that people dislike her boyfriend, the real problem is that she can't see *why*. Once sex enters the picture, it is almost impossible to be objective about a relationship. This is partly because of what sex does to your mind. During sexual arousal, the brain releases a hormone called oxytocin.[5] It works like human superglue because it causes a great emotional bond, increases trust, and makes you less critical of the other person.[6]

Such blinding and binding helps married couples to persevere through tough times. But outside of marriage it can be dangerous. For example, because oxytocin influences you to focus on the positive aspects and memories of the other person, it is easier to overlook the risks of a relationship. One scientist noted, "Oxytocin may affect the extent of these negative evaluations, causing us to say, 'Oh, this won't be too bad.'"[7] Research also shows that intense bonding deactivates the circuits in the brain that are supposed to make judgments about another person![8] This may explain why some people stay in dead-end relationships even though their friends keep warning them to get out. Since estrogen increases the oxytocin response, females experience more intense bonding than men, and suffer more from broken bonds.[9]

When a relationship ends—especially if it is sexual—the couple may feel as if they're experiencing an emotional divorce. In basic terms, sharing the gift of sex is like putting a piece of tape on someone's arm. The first bond is strong, and it will be painful if it is removed. But if you put the same piece of tape on another person's arm, it will be easier to remove. Each time the tape is removed, the bond is weakened because of the leftover residue on the tape. The same is true in relationships, in which previous sexual experiences may interfere with the ability to bond. However, by practicing purity (or starting over if you've made mistakes in the past), you prepare yourself for a greater bond with your future spouse.

These insights may be interesting, but the bottom line is this: Sex outside of marriage doesn't become moral because both people are okay with it. If that were the case, even prostitution could be justified. Just as we did not create ourselves, we do not create the moral law. However, we often want to place ourselves above God when He asks things of us. Pope John Paul II explained this mindset: "If it is convenient and helpful to me, well and good, but if not, I refuse it and leave. . . . Christ is found particularly in the field of sexual morality, because it is here that Christ makes demands on men."[10] Unfortunately, because of our pride, we often don't realize that His laws exist so that our joy might be complete (John 15:11).

If God is the one who created the moral law, why did He reserve sex for marriage? One obvious explanation is that sex makes children, and children belong in families. But there is an even more profound reason, which is written in our own hearts (and bodies): just as people speak a language with their words, they also speak a language with their body. In sex, the body is saying, "I give myself entirely to you. There's nothing of me that I'm not giving to you." But if the couple is not married, then they're speaking a lie with their bodies. They're saying, "I give you my body, but I won't give you myself." Or, "I'm totally yours until I'm totally someone else's." In sex, the body makes a promise, even if you won't. Sex belongs in marriage because only then do the bodies speak the truth: I am yours.

"But what's wrong with sex if the relationship leads to marriage?"

If you hope to marry someone, you obviously want the relationship to last. But are you willing to do what it takes to save your marriage before it starts? Consider this: If a guy gets married as a virgin, his divorce rate is sixty-three percent lower than a non-virgin. For girls, it's seventy-six percent lower.[11] There could be several reasons why virgins have lower divorce rates. One reason, according to the journal *Adolescent and Family Health*, is that, "Those who have premarital sex are more likely to have extramarital sex (affairs)—and extramarital sex contributes to many divorces."[12]

Perhaps a more common reason for the divorce connection is that many sexually active couples make bad marriage decisions because lust causes a false sense of unity. The passion forfeits their ability to look clearly at each other as potential spouses, and the lust can cover up the absence of true love, which never developed between them. Some couples don't intend to use each other, but want to live together or have sex to feel close to each other. However, couples who live together before marriage have a divorce rate nearly eighty percent higher than those who waited until after their wedding to move in together.[13] They're also more than three times as likely to experience infidelity.[14]

If you're going to get married, you'll have the rest of your lives to enjoy sexual intimacy. But now is the only time you'll ever have to prepare for marriage. Consider what makes marriages last: patience, self-control, and sacrifice. Now consider the qualities an abstinent dating couple has to practice: patience, self-control, and sacrifice. When pleasure is valued more than these qualities, couples miss the chance to build the virtues that make love last. After all, being united for life is better than feeling united for a few nights. The fact is: *mutual sacrifice intensifies love*; refusing to sacrifice extinguishes it.

"Is other stuff okay, as long as we don't have sex?"

I know a woman whom I'll call Kate. Her friends were sexually active, so she figured that as long as she kept her virginity, she was good. Kate's boyfriend said that he respected her commitment to virginity, telling her, "I don't want to pressure you to do anything you're not ready for." This made her think that he was a gentleman, and that he loved her. However, he made her feel that she owed him other sexual favors, since she was "holding out" on him. Her girlfriends reminded her that guys have sexual "needs," and that if she wanted to keep him, she'd have to give him something.

Little by little, Kate gave him everything he wanted: except her virginity. She reminded herself that her friends were doing worse things, but she knew she was being used.

Years later, she married someone else and regretted giving in to her ex-boyfriend. Even though she hadn't technically had sex with him, the bond was there, and so were the regrets. This is the bitter fruit that comes from comparing ourselves with those in worse relationships. Look only to Christ, and to how you measure up to His standard. Treat your body as a gift to be guarded jealously, a gift that can be given only with a wedding ring and the lifelong commitment of true love that comes with it.

We always hear about "experimenting" with our sexuality, but you don't "experiment" with something priceless. You experiment with things of little worth that are easily replaced. When we experiment with our bodies and souls, we begin to value them less and less.

"Isn't everybody doing it?"

No. Countless young people have realized the truth about what love is and what sex is worth. They've had their fill of what MTV and *Cosmo* are saying, and they won't be robbed of their chance to have the love God has in mind for them.

Contrary to what the media portrays, teen sexual activity rates have been dropping for over a decade, and now the majority of high school students are virgins.[15] In fact, research shows that the sexual activity rate of high school boys has been dropping twice as quickly as that of high school girls![16] Among those who have already lost their virginity, two-thirds of them wished they had waited longer to have sex (seventy-seven percent of girls and sixty percent of guys).[17] But because of social pressure, even those who are virgins often pretend that they're not. This gives people the impression that everyone is doing it, even though the majority isn't. The pressure also leads some to think of virginity as an embarrassment rather than a gift. But think about it: If your future spouse waited all his or her life to give that gift to you alone, would you feel embarrassed for them, or honored?

"Who would want to save sex for marriage?"

- NFL Quarterback Philip Rivers saved his virginity for marriage, and explained, "It's the greatest gift you could give your wife."
- Former NBA All-Star A. C. Green was also married

as a virgin. He waited because, "I have chosen to follow God's standard, and I've communicated this to my teammates. . . . I have respect for myself and the women I've dated. I try not to focus on idle thoughts that can turn to temptations. . . . I know there's something better for me if I wait."[18] He added, "It is definitely worth waiting. When you marry the right person at the right time you have no regrets. For me, I have nothing but smiles on my face. . . . The first year with the Lakers team my rookie season, they took bets out." He recalls teammates telling him, "There's no way you will be talking abstinence, no way you'll remain a virgin. None of that's possible. Once you see what's going inside the NBA, in the league, you will do everything because these girls are beautiful." Even today, he says, "Most of the guys have come back . . . [and] now they are saying, 'You know what, I sort of wish I had rethought some of my decisions. I wouldn't be in this situation now.'"[19]

- Christie, a high school senior, said this about her potential spouse: "His abstinence from sex is one way to prove his ability to be true to me. I would be so honored to find out that the man I want to marry has respected me enough—without even knowing me—not to have sex with anyone else but me."
- Michael, a twenty-three-year-old, said, "I've had the

opportunity to give away my virginity a few times, but I kept thinking about my future wife. Some people during high school joked about it, but I'm so happy I took the path that I did. When I stand at the altar and lift my wife's veil on our wedding day, who will be laughing then?"

- "I came inches away from losing my virginity at the age of fourteen, on a dark football field, with a guy I barely knew," said a college junior. "I don't know how it happened. I had always been so strong. Then somehow there I was, about to give away my most real possession. I thank God I had the courage to stop, and since that day I've worn a ring to hold the place where my wedding band will go, to remind me of the gift I am saving for my husband."

- Perhaps the greatest reason to practice chastity is also the simplest, offered by an 18-year-old named Matt: "Jesus tells us that the pure of heart will see God. That alone is enough for me."

The more innocence you save, the greater your joy will be to share it on the wedding night. Some disagree, and say that sex is meant for fun. But if that's the case, why do surveys of over one hundred thousand people reveal that married couples who go to church—and especially those who enter marriage with little or no sexual history—have the most satisfying sex lives?[20]

If you think sleeping around will prepare you to be a better spouse, the evidence says the opposite.[21]

One woman said, "I thought I was ready for sex because I felt so in love. It was all based on emotions, and I thought sex would be the way to keep him. But once the relationship ended, sex didn't seem like a big deal. I was 'living in the moment,' and didn't see—or want to admit—what I was doing to myself. Now, years later, I'll be married soon and I wish more than anything that I had waited."

Your virginity was never meant to be "lost," as if it had been misplaced somewhere. It is meant to be given as a gift to the one who deserves it: your spouse. Even if you have lost your virginity, and think this doesn't apply to you, read on. It's never too late.

"What if I'm not a virgin?"

While the loss of virginity has to do with the past, chastity has to do with today. Regardless of what happened last week or last year, you are still worth waiting for. Maybe you lost your virginity, or maybe it was taken from you. Either way, you still have yourself to give. Beginning today, pursue a life of purity.

It's never too late to regain your purity, but the process is challenging. Sometimes it's easy to end bad relationships, but it's tough to keep from jumping back into them. Unfortunately, many who feel like they've given everything away wonder if they have anything left to give. Instead of starting over, they bury one mistake under another so the original wounds won't look so bad. They run from one physical relationship to another, thinking that pleasure will fill their need for love. But this makes the healing process more difficult.

"After I lost my virginity," Crystal confessed, "I didn't respect myself, and one empty relationship led to another. Ever since I was a little girl, I wanted the perfect love, but after all I had done I thought I was the last person on earth to deserve it. Eventually, I realized that finding a good guy wasn't a matter of luck. I started over, raised my standards, and made a commitment to chastity. Now, three years later—and engaged—I haven't regretted a day since."

I remember meeting one girl who slept with fifteen guys in three months. Her schoolmates labeled her a slut. When I asked her why she did this, she said, "Well, it's fun—going to parties and hooking up." I asked her if it really was fun. With tears in her eyes, she answered, "No, it's not. My parents are getting divorced, and there's so much hurt and hate in my family. And just for a minute, when those guys hold me, it feels like love. I know it's not, but at least I feel like somebody wants me." This girl is not a slut. She is a woman with a heart identical to yours and mine, longing for love.

How do you get out of this lifestyle? Well, what advice would you give to your future spouse if right now he or she were sleeping with someone you'll never meet? Follow that same advice, and you'll make it.

In your heart, forgive those who have hurt you, and forgive yourself. We all have things in our past that we wish we could erase. But by practicing chastity in future relationships, you'll see that *living purity will heal the past*. In the meantime, don't assume you always need to be in a relationship. Independence and maturity are attractive qualities.

As a reminder of your commitment and new lifestyle, you could buy a white candle. If you choose to get married one day, you could let your spouse light it on your wedding night.

"Can God forgive you if you've already had sex?"

In the Bible, a woman was caught in sexual sin and taken to Jesus. He didn't condemn her, but defended her from those who were judging her, then forgave her and told her to sin no more (cf. John 8:1–11). His mercy is the same today, so come to the sacraments of reconciliation and then the Eucharist. In reconciliation you'll find God's healing mercy; in the Eucharist, God gives us spiritual nourishment through His body and blood.

Turn with your whole heart to Christ and His immaculate Mother, and they will give you a share in their purity. Offer God your body and your memories, allowing Him to heal you. Because of God's infinite mercy and the fact that purity is a gift from Him, it's never too late to become the person He calls you to be. Every morning His mercies are new (Lam. 3:22–23).

In the words of Mother Teresa, "The devil may try to use the hurts of life, and sometimes our own mistakes, to make you feel it is impossible that Jesus really loves you, is really cleaving to you. This is a danger for all of us. And so sad, because it is completely the opposite of what Jesus is really wanting, waiting to tell you. Not only that He loves you, but even more, He longs for you. He misses you when you don't come close. He thirsts for you. He loves you always, even when you don't feel worthy, when not accepted by others, even by yourself sometimes. He is the one who always accepts you. Only believe that you are precious to Him. Bring all you are suffering to His feet, only open your heart to be loved by Him as you are. He will do the rest."[22]

"If we aren't going to have sex, how far can we go?"

If you're going to get married one day, perhaps someone right now is dating the person you'll eventually marry. How far is too far for them? Practice the purity you would hope your future spouse would have, and treat your dates with the respect that you hope your future spouse would be given. Or consider how you'll expect a guy to treat your daughter one day. By listening to your conscience, you'll know where to draw the line. When we ignore that voice in our heart that tells us right from wrong and give in for the sake of excitement, we end up feeling empty afterward.

So "How far is too far?" is the wrong question. Would you see how close you could come to hitting oncoming traffic while driving? By the time you find out how far is too far, it would be too late. In the same way, we shouldn't ask, "How far can we go toward sin?" Instead, we should think, "How far can we go toward purity?" Perhaps such an idea strikes you as extreme, oppressive, or simply boring. If so, realize that chastity isn't a burden or a list of rules. It's a change of heart: from "getting some" to giving all. As Pope John Paul II said, *the greater the feeling of responsibility you have for your beloved, the more true love there is.*[23]

Sexual passion is supposed to be a good thing. However, igniting sexual passion outside of marriage is like taking fire out of the fireplace and putting it in the living room. Even a good thing can become destructive if it's used in the wrong way. Once the flame of sexual desire is ignited, it's like a fire that doesn't stop burning until everything in its path is consumed. Previous intimacies may become old and the boundaries may often be pushed back to find more excitement and closeness. The couple may even depend on pleasure in order to feel close, and before long, all that may be left is sex. In the long run, their impatient desire for oneness robs them of the opportunity to grow in love, and thus to experience true joy.

When a couple is pure, they still desire to be one. But because of their standards, they choose to channel those powerful desires into creative ways of expressing love. As a result, their friendship and intimacy deepens, and their relationship becomes stronger.

Some people say, "Saving sexual arousal for marriage is too old-fashioned and unrealistic. You need to hook up with at least a few people so you'll have sexual experience. That way, you'll be a greater gift for your spouse on your wedding night." Regardless of a person's sexual history (or lack thereof), we are all worthy of love. But who hopes that their future spouse will amass sexual experiences in order to become a greater gift? Odds are, you would rather your future spouse save his or her first kiss for you. If you would treasure that gift of innocence, why not begin to value your purity as well?

Abstinence isn't just the absence of sex, it's the expression of love. In fact, as a single person, abstinence is a greater expression of love than making love itself, because you're doing what's best for the other person. What was once seen as just "waiting" becomes a time of formation that teaches you how to love. With chastity, even if you aren't dating someone, you can prepare for your future spouse right now by training yourself in faithfulness.

"What if I want to be free to do whatever I want?"

You want freedom? How about no longer worrying about questions like "Will I get a disease? Will my parents find out? Will we get pregnant? Am I being used?" Freed from these problems, you'll be free to love—without anxiety about the future or regrets about the past. This is true freedom: the ability to do what's right.

You're right to desire freedom, because freedom makes love possible. But realize that chastity isn't the loss of freedom; it's the fulfillment of it. A person who is controlled by his hormones is not free. He isn't giving himself to a woman or loving her, but using her as an outlet for his sexual "needs." While lust blinds us and distorts our desires, purity liberates us. After all, we don't become free by doing whatever we want. We become free—and able to love—when we have self-control. Until then, we're slaves chained to birth control, since we lack the freedom of self-control.

"Won't chastity ruin the excitement of dating?"

Not in the least. Chastity does away with the mind games often played to get someone into bed. Sadly, many women give sex to men for the sake of getting "love," while the men often seem to give "love" for the sake of getting sex. Your heart—and the gift of sex—is made for something better than that.

After all, giving in to one's hormones is not romance. It is lust, and while it may be spontaneous and temporarily exciting, using another person isn't romantic. In fact, too many good, romantic relationships have been ruined by lust.

Sometimes a person's actions may appear romantic because they're so imaginative and thoughtful, but the actions may be done to manipulate or seduce the other. This is not romance, because love is absent. Only when purity is present can one tell the difference between loving romance and selfish seduction. If you inform your date that you won't sleep with him or her, and that person leaves you—then you know immediately what you were being "loved" for. If you're looking for excitement, knowing that you're loved is much more exciting than wondering if you're being used.

Purity doesn't mean being a prude. It means that you have the strength to conquer lust so that you're free to fall in love for the right reasons. Purity doesn't mean you have a negative or unhealthy view of sex. You just know how much it's worth, and you realize that *if you give it away for free, you're saying that it isn't worth anything.* In the words of one woman, "when you put on chastity, you'll discover a life more hope-filled, more vibrant, more real than anything you might have experienced while having sex outside of marriage. That is the thrill of the chaste."[24]

"What about pornography? I'm not hurting anyone."

Pornography trains people to measure the value of others based upon how much lust we feel for them. We may jokingly try to convince ourselves that it isn't a problem, but our ability to love is being crippled. While we're busy fantasizing, our masculinity and femininity becomes warped, and if we enter into real relationships, we'll make the frustrating mistake of confusing love with lust. While love involves sacrifice and commitment, pornography teaches us to reduce others to sexual objects that can be used and then discarded once our passion wears off. We're made for love, but we can't love a fantasy and it can't love us.

Although pornography isn't just a male problem, consider how it affects men: When a man loves a woman, he loves her for who she is. Such love is impossible with pornography because the man "loves" only what she gives him. He has no idea who the woman is. This is why Pope John Paul II said that the problem with pornography is not that it shows too *much*, but that it shows too *little*. It shows too little because it reduces a woman to her body parts. Instead of inviting you to manhood, pornography trains you to reject responsibility for a woman. Referring to Web sites and magazines as "adult" or to a strip joint as a "gentleman's club" couldn't be further from the truth. Women know that real men don't indulge in either. After all, what kind of guy needs to pay money so that a woman will pretend that she likes him?

Some argue that porn is just a harmless way to relieve temptations. But pornography doesn't get rid of temptations any more than prostitution does. As Christians, our goal isn't to get rid of sexual desire but to master our desires for the sake of love. The idea that pornography can be used to decrease temptation is like saying that lighter fluid can be used to extinguish a fire.

Lastly, *pornography is the perfect way to ruin your future marriage*. It trains the brain to associate sex with dirty, illicit, sexual fantasies of countless disposable women. And even though it takes only a few seconds to see the pictures, it takes years to forget them. This causes tremendous strain in marriage, because the spouse is compared to the models and is expected to provide as much excitement. When this doesn't happen, the couple suffers and the spouse feels hurt and unable to "live up" to the fantasies. Who wants to put his or her future bride or groom through this?

In the words of one husband, pornography causes "those distortions of our sexual desires that we must struggle against in order to discover true love."[25] So if you own pornography, for the love of your future spouse, trash it immediately. To the degree you love women, fight pornography.

"What about masturbation?"

God created sex for two purposes: bonding and babies. Masturbation achieves neither, and instead of communicating life and love, the purpose of sex becomes the satisfaction of lust. By looking to yourself for sexual fulfillment, the center of the sexual act becomes "me" instead of "we." In other words, it trains you in selfishness. Just as purity teaches you to give, masturbation teaches you to take. It incites lustful thoughts, and leads you to believe that you deserve—and need—sexual gratification whenever the desire arises. However, nothing bad happens to a man's body if he isn't sexually active.

Love is a gift of self, but you cannot give what you do not possess. If you don't have self-control, you can't truly give yourself to another. If a person can't conquer his habit of lust, then how will he love a spouse one day? Instead of using his fantasies for sexual gratification, he'll use his wife.

Though sexual sins are highly tempting, God's grace is stronger. Like any other serious sin, they can be overcome with patience, perseverance, and love—not to mention prayer and fasting. Keep your eyes on Jesus, who will complete the good work He began in you (cf. Phil. 1:6).

"Is homosexuality a sin?"

The causes of homosexual attractions have not been fully explained, and many who experience these temptations do not choose or want them. People with same-sex attractions are called to a life of chastity along with the rest of the members of the Church who battle with their own temptations. By living in God's grace, they can and should approach Christian perfection. Others must treat them not as outcasts but with respect and compassion, for, as Jesus said, "As you did it to one of the least of these my brethren, you did it to me" (Matt. 25:40).

The media tells people that if they experience a same-sex attraction, this means that they were born gay, that they need to come out and embrace this lifestyle, and that anyone who doesn't approve of homosexual behavior is bigoted against them. The fact is that the genetic evidence for homosexuality is inconclusive. But this is beside the point. People shouldn't be labeled by their sexual attractions, as if that were their identity. They are sons and daughters of God, and *that* is their identity.

While it's not a sin to have homosexual temptations, it is a sin to indulge in homosexual acts. This may be hard to understand today, because society tells us that sex equals love and that it's fine to separate sex from creating life. However, God designed the sexual act for a sacred purpose. He joined lovemaking with life giving, and what God has joined, no one must separate. When we understand sex for what it is—a reflection of God's life-giving love—it becomes clear that same-sex unions cannot reflect this. Members of the same sex can reflect his love by doing what is best for each other, but the sexual act must always be ordered toward giving life.

If you experience same-sex attractions, realize that you're not alone and that the Church has a network to encourage and strengthen you: www.couragerc.net.

"What about safe sex?"

There is no such thing. In fact, the very concept of "Safe Sex" is degrading. For one, it equates us with animals that need to be neutered because they have no self-control. Secondly, it reduces human sexuality to a merely genital act because it implies that people are "safe" when their risk of infection and pregnancy is decreased. Shouldn't we be concerned about protecting the entire person, including the heart and soul, instead of just the reproductive organs? All of this is impacted by sexual activity, but seems to be ignored by those who call sex with a condom "safe." Thirdly, it gives people a license to use others by enjoying the pleasures of sex without permanent commitment. By encouraging people to be "protected" instead of respected, those who support "safe sex" are causing the problems they pretend to solve. For example, here are the statistics you never hear:

- Human papilloma virus (HPV) is the most common STD in the world.[26] It causes 99.7 percent of cervical cancer,[27] and this kills more than 288,000 women each year![28] So, with each sexual partner a woman has, her risk of cervical cancer increases. Your body, like your heart, isn't made for multiple sexual partners. It's made for enduring love.
- While condom use may reduce the risk of HPV-related diseases, it doesn't offer much protection from HPV, because the virus is spread by skin-to-skin contact throughout the entire genital area, including one's thighs and lower abdomen.[29] How large is the problem? The Centers for Disease Control reported that *the majority of sexually active women have been infected with one or more types of genital HPV*.[30] Good luck finding that on the warning label of a condom!

- If you have sex with a person, you're basically having sex with everyone he or she had sex with, not to mention the others their partners have had sex with. By having sexual contact with one person, you could be exposing yourself to the STDs of hundreds of people.[31] This is frightening, considering that eighty percent of people who have an STD are unaware of their own infection.[32] For example, a person who has the HIV virus may not show symptoms of AIDS for up to ten years.
- Oral sex can transmit virtually every STD,[33] and hand-to-genital contact can transmit some as well.[34] So even virgins can get STDs,[35] including oral cancer, from HPV.[36]
- If a woman gets chlamydia and isn't treated in time, she may become infertile. Seventy-five percent of women (and fifty percent of men) don't show symptoms after they contract it.[37] Thus, it is called "the silent sterilizer." *Think, girls: Is this guy worth losing your ability to have kids?*
- Most STDs can be carried into marriage undetected. For example, ninety percent of people with genital herpes do not know that they are infected.[38] In the case of HPV, it will often clear up on its own. But when a husband is infected with it, his wife is five times as likely to get cervical cancer.[39]
- Several STDs are incurable, and many can be passed

on from a mother to her baby. This can cause brain damage, blindness, deafness, pneumonia, liver disease, and even death in the newborn.

- One out of every six teenage girls will become pregnant during her first year of using birth control.[40] That's why even Planned Parenthood's research institute had to admit that most high school pregnancies are caused by contraceptive failure, not by the failure to use them.[41] Now consider that a woman can get pregnant only a few days of the month—but you can get an STD any day.

- Birth control pills interfere with a woman's immune system,[42] making her more likely to contract certain STDs.[43] Among countless other side effects, the pill increases a woman's chance of having breast cancer,[44] cervical cancer,[45] liver cancer,[46] and potentially fatal blood clots.[47]

- The shot (Depo-Provera) and the patch (Ortho Evra) carry similar risks, or worse.[48] That's why the makers of the patch are facing lawsuits related to deaths and other injuries from at least 1000 women.[49] Meanwhile, women have sued the makers of the shot for $700 million![50] One reason for this is because the shot thins out a woman's bones.[51] This is especially worrisome for young women, because the teenage years are a critical time for bone development. After years of receiving birth control injections as a teen, a girl in her early twenties could have the bones of a fifty to sixty-year-old. Interestingly, because of its link to breast cancer, veterinarians stopped prescribing Depo-Provera for dogs.[52] However, it's still being given to women, and is sometimes injected into male sex offenders to decrease their sex drive![53]

- Many women are told that hormonal birth control (the pill, the shot, or the patch) will prevent pregnancy. While this is true some of the time, these drugs can also allow conception to occur, and then abort the newly conceived baby before the mother is aware of the pregnancy.[54] The same is true of the morning-after pill.[55]

- When birth control fails, many are offered abortion as a solution, and are told that their life will return to normal after the procedure. However, these women often experience depression, and are six times more likely to commit suicide than women who gave birth.[56]

- It is not God's plan for couples to sterilize acts of love. In fact, while half of all marriages end in divorce, couples who use Natural Family Planning have a divorce rate of less than two percent.[57]

These statistics are not listed in order to frighten you. They've been included so that you will be better able to love. Once you understand the design of your body, you'll see that you were created to live in a certain way. When we veer from that design, we often harm ourselves and others. But by practicing chastity, you not only protect yourself, *you protect your future spouse and children if you do get married.*

To get tested for an STD, or to find post-abortion healing for guys as well as girls, call a crisis pregnancy center. They'll tell you where to go, and it's usually free. Don't put this off because of fear. If the clinic offers you birth control, you can decline, because you have self-control.

You might wonder, "If I can't use a condom, then how am I supposed to protect myself?" For one, *you can know that it isn't love if you feel the need to protect yourself from your beloved.* You protect yourself from enemies. You receive your beloved without reserve. If you aren't married and aren't ready to receive that person fully, then it's not time to give him or her your body. We weren't designed to be given in pieces.

To express how tremendous the act of lovemaking is, God uses it to bring an eternal soul into the world. The act cries out for permanence. By his or her existence, that child is saying, "I'm permanent, so you two should be as well!"

Often, the couple knows that they're not ready for the total giving and commitment their bodies are promising, so they deny the natural process of life-giving love. They treat pregnancy as a disease against which they must be protected or vaccinated, instead of a gift to receive with joy.

"What if I'm sexually active now?"

Stop the sexual activity, and consider whether you're a better person because of the relationship. Or is it turning you into someone you never wanted to be? Don't remain in the relationship to be a hero or to rescue the other person. You'll only end up getting hurt. You might need to break up, but at least take some time away. If the person loves you, he or she will give you as much time and space as you need. And if this is real love, then taking a break won't hurt.

Take time to pray, and ask yourself if your boyfriend (or girlfriend) is saying, "I won't wait for you. If you love me you'd sleep with me now"? Or "I want the best for you, and I know our love is strong enough to save that gift until marriage"? If your date won't do what's best for you before marriage, don't expect things to change in marriage. *You won't miss out on love if you leave a dead-end relationship.* The only way you'll miss out on love is if you stay, blindly hoping that things will miraculously improve.

Instead, make a firm decision, as this sixteen-year-old did: "No more baggage, no alcohol, no drugs, no excuses, no hasty rationalizations, no lies, just pure love.

I think that's what I've been looking for this whole time. I have to stop running away from the person that God wants me to be." So make this decision for yourself, go to the sacrament of reconciliation, and trust that the Lord has something better in store for you.

"How do I say 'no'?"

If you want love, then the most important word you need to learn is "no." By saying no to the cheap imitations of love, you're really saying "yes" to the real thing. When you need to draw the line, be clear, confident, and firm. Be sure to say "no" with your words and your body language. If you are lying on a couch with your date and whispering a half-hearted "no," he or she probably won't take you seriously, since you don't take yourself seriously.

If your heart says, "Maybe I shouldn't be doing this," listen to that intuition, pray for strength, and get out of the situation. How? Any way that will work: Say that you respect the other person too much to do that with him or her. Or say that you don't feel comfortable, that you need to get home. Or blame it on your parents. I heard of one girl who said to her date, "Here's my cell phone. Call my dad, and if he says it's okay, then I'm ready to go." Better yet, say that only your future spouse deserves to get that close to you, and then only after you're married. Most of all, don't be afraid to look a person in the eye and say, "no." If you freely give your body to others, it commands no respect because there's dullness in a person who is unable to set standards and have the character to stick to them. On the other hand, people commit for life to those who respect themselves.

If you want to avoid hurting the other's feelings, compliment him or her on why you enjoy being together. Then explain how purity unites a couple better than passion. This shows that you aren't pushing him or her away, but are seeking a deeper love. But realize that you don't owe your date a thirty-minute lecture on why chastity is important to you. If your date loves you, then he or she won't pressure you. This is the real test to see if you are being loved or used. "Love waits to give, but lust can't wait to get."[58]

"How do I avoid mistakes in the future?"

Avoid situations where mistakes often happen, such as being alone together at home, in the back room of a party, or on a bed. The situation may seem harmless, but can result in something as serious as date rape. Avoid drugs and alcohol, which are the gateway to many regrets. These can influence you to do things that you would otherwise reject. Some people use them for just this reason: so that they can blame the substances for their own behavior.

It's one thing to avoid a bad situation, and it's another to avoid a bad relationship. Take time to build a friendship first. Know your standards and make sure your date knows them, too. Don't pursue a relationship with a person who wears down your morals and will physically take from you everything that you're willing to give. You deserve better. Another wise move is to date only someone you can see yourself marrying. If we get involved in relationships that we know won't last, we're training ourselves for divorce.

Now I'd like to say a word to young women hoping for love. This may not be fun to hear, but keep in mind that I say this as a guy in my twenties: During your teenage years, stay away from older guys.

Here's why: seventy-four percent of girls who lose their virginity as teens lose it to an older guy.[59] In fact, the majority of teen pregnancies are caused by older guys.[60] Why do so many young women fall into this trap? One reason is because girls mature sooner than boys do. A teenage girl may be bored with the maturity level of guys her own age. Older guys realize this, and have more refined "grooming techniques" to flatter girls with their attention. For example, he may give her a promise ring and tell her they'll be together forever, so that she'll think any sexual activity they share is more special. Distractions like this quiet the girl's intuitions, which are probably screaming at her to stay away from him.

Older guys also use lines like, "I've never felt this way about a girl before . . . but I'm okay if you don't want to have sex." Some girls melt at hearing this because they think the guy really wants what's best for them. In reality, he probably doesn't have enough social skills to date a girl his own age, and he figures that a naive younger girl is less likely to have the maturity and confidence to turn him down. It's not the girl's job to be the "chastity cop," but a man will be as much of a gentleman as a woman requires. Obviously, not all older guys are bad, but if he's as good as you think he is, why hasn't a girl his own age snatched him up by now?

Also, ask yourself, "What is my body worth?" Is it for sale at the price of a movie and dinner? No matter how much a guy spends on the date, you're not obligated to offer him your body. Remember that anyone who breaks up with you because you don't give in to his lust isn't worthy of your attention to begin with.

A word for the guys: Don't wait for the girl to stop. St. Paul tells husbands that they should imitate Christ, who was willing to die to save His bride, the Church, from sin (cf. Eph. 5:25–26). The same must be true of a young man seeking a spouse. A real man guards a woman's innocence instead of seeking ways to empty her of it. He carries her soul into the arms of God, not into the slavery of sin. It's no coincidence that the word virtue comes from a Latin root meaning "manly strength." When a man practices the virtue of chastity, he becomes more masculine. According to one college woman, "Being able to have sex isn't what makes a boy into a man. Anyone can have sex. It's the ability to have self-control that sets the men apart from the boys." So realize that *women seek Jesus in a man*, because He is the model of selfless love. Real men live and love like Jesus, desiring heaven for women.

"Does how I dress make a difference in how a guy treats me?"

Women deserve unconditional respect no matter what they wear. However, the way a girl dresses (and dances) sends a message to men. If her sexual value is the first impression she gives to a man, she'll be more likely to encounter the type of guys who want to use her body. They might say or do whatever is necessary to get access to it. But after she gives in, they often lose respect for her, get bored, and leave. Meanwhile, she's left thinking, "Maybe if I had been skinnier, or had done more with him sexually, he would have liked me more and stayed longer." No, but he may have used her longer. The ultimate cause of this was not her outfit, but rather the failure of the man and the woman to treat each other with love. But if a woman yearns to be treated with such reverence, then she cannot afford to forget that she has power in the way she presents herself to men.

Modesty is a bold statement of your worth because it invites men to consider something deeper about you. It tells a guy that he can take you seriously as a woman, because you don't need to make boys gawk at you in order to feel secure. I'll grant that guys will stare at a girl who wears a short skirt that could be mistaken for a wide belt. But none of them respect her more because of it. As a woman, do you long to be gawked at or to be loved?

If your heart is saying, "Is this too short?" or "Is this too tight?" listen to that intuition because it has answered your question. Stand in front of a mirror and ask, "What am I drawing attention to with this outfit? Is this outfit saying that the best thing about me is my body, or does it announce that I'm worth waiting to see?"

Modesty does not mean looking unattractive or covering every inch of your body as if it's bad or dirty. Like a bride wearing a veil, clothing conceals a woman's body as an invitation of respect. Your body is a tabernacle for life and a temple of the Holy Spirit, not a collection of body parts. But if you don't realize this about yourself, how will a man?

A woman's most fascinating trait is the mystery of her femininity. Men find it captivating, and it is something to guard at all costs. Modesty preserves this mystery, since *nothing adorns a woman with as much beauty as purity does.* In the words of Archbishop Fulton J. Sheen, "The beauty on the outside never gets into the soul. But the beauty of the soul reflects itself on the face."[61] Modest dress manifests pure womanhood, and this is the first line of defense for the virtue of chastity. Realize that purity is attractive. After all, you're not *playing* hard to get—you *are* hard to get.

"If a guy has a bad imagination, isn't that his problem?"

It is his problem. But when a woman gets frustrated because men don't respect her, it becomes her problem, too. That's why modesty is called the guardian of love. When a guy meets a woman who respects herself, he knows that if he wants to enjoy her company, he'll need to be a gentleman.

If you want to find a man of character, realize that he isn't looking for a girl who dresses provocatively. Unfortunately, the media tells women that the less they wear, the more guys will like them. Girls are also led to believe that their bodies are never perfect enough, and that if they want love, they have to look like the starving airbrushed models in fashion magazines (who, by the way, never seem to have perfect relationships). With such unrealistic pressures, women often fail to realize that they're already made in the image and likeness of God, and they need not look like goddesses in order to deserve love. When a girl focuses so much on the physical aspect, she may overlook the qualities a virtuous guy would hope to find in her: faithfulness, honesty, and respect.

You may be thinking, "That sounds great, but where are these ideal men hiding?" Well, I've met countless young men who wonder the same thing about modest women. It's almost as if we're so concerned about what others think that we're too afraid to be ourselves. We've become so obsessed with the opinions of others that we ignore the will of God.

Most women don't dress to incite lustful thoughts. If anything, they're more concerned about what other women will think of their outfit! However, a woman who desires love shoots herself in the foot if she dresses immodestly. She may think that her outfit is cute, but trust me—he's not looking at her outfit. Instead, his lust is separating him from Jesus. What woman wants to remove men from the model of unconditional love? Even though men generally don't like to ask for help, when it comes to having a pure mind, we need the help of our sisters in Christ. Pope John Paul II said, "Men must be taught to love, and to love in a noble way; they must be educated in depth in this truth, that is, in the fact that a woman is a person and not simply an object."[62]

Some women are so busy trying to turn a guy's head that they never realize they have the power to turn a guy's heart. Girls, *do not underestimate your power to change the way the world looks at sex and the dignity of womanhood.*

"How do I stay pure?"

First of all, don't let the fear of rejection control your relationships. Many young women are afraid of offending or losing their boyfriends if they don't yield to their sexual demands. One woman said, "So often girls think, 'I have to do it to please him,' but later they feel awful, particularly when he runs off with another girl."[63] These insecurities must be overcome if you are ever to be loved as you deserve. Instead of worrying about him leaving if you don't give him something sexual, let him worry about you leaving unless he respects you!

Similarly, many guys are afraid that a girl will think less of them if they turn down her sexual advances. But if a girl is pressuring you, it might be because she is afraid you will ignore or reject her if she doesn't offer you something sexual.

Besides guarding your body, guard your mind as well. As St. Paul said, "Whatever is honorable, whatever is just, whatever is pure . . . think about these things" (Phil. 4:8). So, don't warp your imagination with sensual TV shows, websites, movies, magazines, gossip, or music that glorifies meaningless sex. Some people justify their enjoyment of these things by saying that they're not affected by them. This is like thinking that you won't be stained by rolling in tar. If you are serious about love, get rid of these things. Ask yourself: "Is it that I couldn't be trying any more to avoid lust, or that I couldn't be trying any less?"

"As a guy, isn't having a pure mind impossible?"

Having sexual desires isn't bad. It's normal. But we must control our imagination, cleanse our speech, and avoid looking at girls as objects. Jesus said, "Everyone who looks at a woman lustfully has already committed adultery with her in his heart" (Matt. 5:28). But Pope John Paul II says we should not fear the severity of these words but have confidence in their power to save us.[64] Christ did not come simply to redeem our souls, but to redeem our bodies and even our desires. There's a battle between love and lust in all of us. But by becoming men of prayer, we'll conquer temptations and learn to love women instead of using them.

If you've ever wrestled, you know that your opponent's body will follow where you direct his head. The same is true of your mind. Control your sexual thoughts and you will gain discipline over your body. When a sexual temptation comes to mind, stop and pray for purity, then pray for the person.

The more you practice chastity, the easier it becomes, and the better you'll prepare yourself for love. For example, when men are pure, they learn how to show true love and affection. A man becomes a better lover since he learns to love the whole woman, not just her body. Chastity is not the absence of temptation, but the victory of love over it.

That's why the need for chastity does not end when you get married. Chastity is the capacity to love another and have reverence for the gift of sexuality no matter what your state in life: married, single, or religious. Although abstinence ends for couples who marry, chastity holds them together. If you're sick of divorce and you hope that if you do get married it will last, start living the virtue of chastity today.

"How is purity possible?"

Purity is a gift from Jesus Christ, and He will give it to us if we ask for it with humility and perseverance. Without Him, it is impossible. But in the words of Pope John Paul II, love is "victorious because it prays."[65] According to St. Paul, we "can do all things in Him who strengthens" us (Phil. 4:13).

God is always present to give you His grace, or to witness when you turn from Him. But don't think of God as some divine killjoy, constantly looking over your shoulder to make sure you don't enjoy yourself.

He loves you beyond what you could ever imagine, and He wants what's best for you. He longs to see you truly alive and happy, but sin doesn't fit into that picture.

To be pure, follow the advice of Blessed Pier Giorgio Frassati: "With all the strength of my soul I urge you young people to approach the Communion table as often as you can. Feed on this bread of angels whence you will draw all the energy you need to fight inner battles. Because true happiness, dear friends, does not consist in the pleasures of the world or in earthly things, but in peace of conscience, which we have only if we are pure in heart and mind."[66]

If you want grace, spend time with Jesus in prayer, go to Mass and confession, pray the rosary daily, read the Bible, ask St. Joseph and the saints and your guardian angel to pray for you, pray the stations of the cross, go to adoration of the Blessed Sacrament, and find a holy friend or priest with whom you can talk.

If we don't pick up these weapons and yet complain that purity is too difficult, it is as if we are waving a white flag of surrender while sitting on a tank. We are not helpless. Either we'll stop the prayers or the prayers will stop the sin. They cannot last long together, so persevere in prayer. *Especially with true devotion to the Blessed Virgin Mary, anyone can obtain the purity that is a requirement of real love.* Keep fighting the good fight. The heavenly crown and your future spouse are well worth it!

"What does God say?"

God never waters down the truth, but speaks it to us in love. Below are your questions, and His answers.

Q: What is real love?
A: "Love is patient and kind; love is not jealous or boastful. It is not arrogant or rude. Love does not insist on its own way; it is not irritable or resentful; it does not rejoice at wrong, but rejoices in the right. Love bears all things, believes all things, hopes all things, endures all things" (1 Cor. 13:4–7).

Q: Will impurity really affect my relationship with God?
A: "Blessed are the pure in heart, for they shall see God" (Matt. 5:8). "He who loves purity of heart, and whose speech is gracious, will have the king as his friend" (Prov. 22:11).

Q: What's so bad about impurity?
A: "Do not be deceived; neither the immoral . . . nor adulterers . . . nor drunkards . . . will inherit the kingdom of God. . . . The body is not meant for immorality, but for the Lord, and the Lord for the body. . . . Shun immorality. Every other sin which a man commits is outside the body; but the immoral man sins against his own body. Do you not know that your body is a temple of the Holy Spirit within you, which you have from

God? You are not your own; you were bought with a price. So glorify God in your body" (1 Cor. 6:9–20).

Q: But could God ever forgive me?
A: "As the heavens tower over the earth, so God's love towers over the faithful. As far as the east is from the west, so far have our sins been removed from us" (Ps. 103:11–12, *NAB*).

Q: What is God's will for me?
A: "This is the will of God, your holiness: that you refrain from immorality, that each of you know how to acquire a wife for himself in holiness and honor, not in lustful passion . . . For God did not call us to impurity but to holiness. Therefore, whoever disregards this, disregards not a human being but God, who gives His holy Spirit to you" (1 Thess. 4:3–8, *NAB*). "For I know well the plans I have in mind for you . . . plans for your welfare, not for woe! plans to give you a future full of hope. When you call me, when you go to pray to me, I will listen to you. When you look for me, you will find me. Yes, when you seek me with all your heart, you will find me with you . . . and I will change your lot" (Jer. 29:11–14, *NAB*). See also: Rom. 12:2 and 1 Tim. 4:12.

"What do I do now?"

Don't be passive, but prepare for real love. One way

to do this is to enjoy being single. Most teens are under such pressure to constantly have a boyfriend or girlfriend that they never have the time or space to discover their own identity and dreams. Or, they feel as if there is something defective about them because they are not in a relationship. Don't fall for this. As one high school girl said to me, "You don't go through high school looking for your husband. You go through high school looking for your bridesmaids." Follow her advice, and hang out with friends who support your lifestyle instead of wearing it down.

In your relationships, set your standards high, because you'll get what you'll settle for. If you need to lower them to date someone, something is wrong. Write down the standards that you hope your spouse will meet. After writing the list, read it and ask yourself: "By the way I'm living today, do I deserve this person?" If not, begin to become one who does.

If you feel called to marriage, pray for your future spouse, that he or she will be preserved from the deception of sin, and know that the Lord will join you both when He knows best. While some are called to the married life, others are invited to make a total gift of themselves in the priesthood or religious life. Which is meant for you? As sensuality clouds our judgment, purity helps us to see our relationships and even our vocation with clarity. Even if you don't plan to marry or enter religious life, you won't regret this decision to respect yourself and honor God.

Some of the best things in life are obtained through trial and suffering. As Pope John Paul II reminded us, "Love between man and woman cannot be built without sacrifices and self-denial."[67] But do not be afraid when love makes demands on you, because you have been created for such love—and you will not be satisfied with anything less. If you want love to be as good as it gets, you must persevere. You have everything to gain, and you will have no more regrets. *Purity knows no regrets.* The devil promises much, but gives nothing. God invites you on a difficult path, but will give you more than you ever imagined.

In an age in which people expect instant gratification, chastity proclaims a challenge of sacrifice and patience. It's a battle. But God would never call you to a lifestyle without giving you the grace to live it. Know that this purity of mind, heart, and body is possible. As a twenty-seven-year-old virgin engaged to Crystal, the woman whose quote is toward the top of page 17, I know it is possible—and well worth it!

Daily Prayer to Mary

Mary, loving daughter of God the Father, I give my soul to your care. Protect the life of God in my soul. Do not let me lose it by sin. Protect my mind and my will so that all my thoughts and desires will be pleasing to God.

Hail Mary, full of grace, the Lord is with thee. Blessed art thou among women, and blessed is the fruit of thy womb, Jesus. Holy Mary, Mother of God, pray for us sinners, now and at the hour of our death. Amen.

Mary, loving Mother of God the Son, I give my heart to your care. Let me love you with all my heart. Let me always try to love my neighbor. And help me avoid friends who might lead me away from Jesus and into a life of sin. *Hail Mary . . .*

Mary, loving spouse of the Holy Spirit, I give my body to your care. Let me always remember that my body is a home for the Holy Spirit who dwells in me. Let me never sin against Him by any impure actions alone or with others, against the virtue of purity.

Hail Mary . . .

St. Joseph, pray for us.
St. Raphael the Archangel, pray for us.
St. Maria Goretti, pray for us.
Amen.

Listen to our **Podcast**

Follow us on:

chastity.com/connect

GOT QUESTIONS? GET ANSWERS.

WATCH VIDEOS
GET RELATIONSHIP ADVICE
LAUNCH A PROJECT
READ ANSWERS TO TOUGH QUESTIONS
FIND HELP TO HEAL FROM THE PAST
LISTEN TO POWERFUL TESTIMONIES
SHOP FOR GREAT RESOURCES
SCHEDULE A SPEAKER

1   Karol Wojtyła, *Love and Responsibility* (San Francisco: Ignatius Press, 1993), 134.

2   S. Ryan, et al., "The First Time: Characteristics of Teens' First Sexual Relationships," *Research Brief* (Washington, DC: Child Trends, August, 2003), 5.

3   Josh McDowell and Dick Day, *Why Wait: What You Need to Know about the Teen Sexuality Crisis* (San Bernardino, CA: Here's Life Publishers, 1987).

4   Meg Meeker, M.D., *Epidemic: How Teen Sex Is Killing Our Kids* (Washington, DC: Lifeline Press, 2002), 78.

5   Carmichael, et al., "Plasma oxytocin increases in the human sexual response," *The Journal of Clinical Endocrinology and Metabolism* 64:1 (January 1987): 27-31; Murphy, et al., "Changes in oxytocin and vasopressin secretion during sexual activity in men," *The Journal of Clinical Endocrinology and Metabolism* 65:4 (October 1987): 738-741.

6   Kosfeld, et al., "Oxytocin increases trust in humans," *Nature* 435 (2005): 673-676; Heinrichs, et al., "Selective amnesic effects of oxytocin on human memory," *Physiology & Behavior* 83 (2004): 31–38; Bartz, et al., "The neuroscience of affiliation: Forging links between basic and clinical research on neuropeptides and social behavior," *Hormones and Behavior* 50 (2006): 518–528; B. Ditzen, "Effects of Social Support and Oxytocin on Psychological and Physiological Stress Responses during Marital Conflict," International Congress Of Neuroendocrinology, Pittsburgh, PA: June 19–22, 2006; Crenshaw, M.D., *The Alchemy of Love and Lust* (New York: Pocket Books, 1996).

7   E. Svoboda, "Inhaled 'Cuddle' Hormone Promotes Trust," *Discover* 27:1 (January 2006): 56.

8   Bartels and Zeki, "The neural correlates of maternal and romantic love," *NeuroImage* 21 (2004): 1155–1166.

9   Cf. Pfaff, et al., "Neural Oxytocinergic Systems as Genomic Targets for Hormones and as Modulators of Hormone-Dependant Behaviors," *Results and Problems in Cell Differentiation* 26 (1999): 91-105, as quoted by Eric J. Keroack, M.D., and John R. Diggs, Jr., M.D., "Bonding Imperative," A Special Report from the Abstinence Medical Council (Abstinence Clearinghouse, April 30, 2001); K. Joyner and R. Udry, "You Don't Bring Me Anything but Down: Adolescent Romance and Depression," *Journal of Health and Social Behavior* 41:4 (December 2000): 361-391; Hallfors, et al., "Which Comes First in Adolescence—Sex and Drugs or Depression?" *American Journal of Preventive Medicine* 29:3 (2005): 163-170.

10 Karol Wojtyła, *The Way to Christ* (San Francisco: Harper, 1994), 55.

11 Edward O. Laumann, et al., *The Social Organization of Sexuality: Sexual Practices in the United States* (Chicago: University of Chicago Press, 1994), 503.

12 R. Finger, et al., "Association of Virginity at Age 18 with Educational, Economic, Social, and Health Outcomes in Middle Adulthood," *Adolescent & Family Health* 3:4 (2004): 169.

13 Cf. Bennett, et. al., "Commitment and the Modern Union: Assessing the Link Between Premarital Cohabitation and Subsequent Marital Stability," *American Sociological Review* 53:1 (February 1988): 127-138.

14 Forste, et al., "Sexual Exclusivity Among Dating, Cohabiting, and Married Women," *Journal of Marriage and the Family* 58:1 (1996): 43.

15 Centers for Disease Control, "Youth Risk Behavior Surveillance—United States, 2005,"

Morbidity and Mortality Weekly Report 55:SS-5 (June 9, 2006): 19.

16   Cf. Centers for Disease Control, "Trends in HIV-Related Behaviors Among High School Students — United States 1991-2005," *Morbidity and Mortality Weekly Report* 55:31 (August 11, 2006): 851-854.

17   National Campaign to Prevent Teen Pregnancy, *America's Adults and Teens Sound Off About Teen Pregnancy: An Annual National Survey* (December 16, 2003), 17.

18   Foundation for the Family, *Practicing Teen Chastity* (Cincinnati, OH: Couple to Couple League).

19   "NBA Ironman Proud to Be a Virgin Until 38," http://abcnews.go.com/GMA/story?id=125643&page=1, October 29, 2002.

20   Cf. William R. Mattox, Jr., "Aha! Call it the revenge of the church ladies," *USA TODAY*, February 11, 1999, 15-A.

21   Cf. William R. Mattox Jr., "The Hottest Valentines: The Startling Secret of What Makes You a High-Voltage Lover," *The Washington Post*, February 13, 1994.

22   Michael Collopy, *Works of Love are Works of Peace* (San Francisco: Ignatius Press, 1996), 197.

23   Cf. Karol Wojtyła, *Love and Responsibility*, 131.

24   Dawn Eden, *The Thrill of the Chaste* (Nashville, TN: W Publishing Group, 2006), xii.

25   Christopher West, *Good News about Sex and Marriage* (Ann Arbor, MI: Charis Books, 2000), 84.

26   Cf. Martinon-Torres, et al., "Human papillomavirus vaccines: A new challenge for pediatricians," *Anales de Pediatría* 65:5 (November 2006): 461-469; Trottier, et al., "The epidemiology of genital human papillomavirus infection,"*Vaccine* 24:S1 (March 2006): 4; Division of STD Prevention, "Prevention of Genital HPV Infection and Sequelae: Report of an External Consultants' Meeting," Department of Health and Human Services, Atlanta: Centers for Disease Control and Prevention (CDC) (December 1999): 1.

27   Cf. J. M. Walboomers, et al., "Human Papillomavirus Is a Necessary Cause of Invasive Cervical Cancer Worldwide," *Journal of Pathology* 189:1 (September 1999): 12–19.

28   World Health Organization, International Agency for Research on Cancer, 2006, www.iarc.fr.

29   Cf. National Institutes of Health, "Scientific Evidence on Condom Effectiveness for Sexually Transmitted Disease (STD) Prevention" (June 2000) 26, www.niaid.nih.gov/dmid/stds/condomreport.pdf; House of Representatives, "Breast and Cervical Cancer Prevention and Treatment Act of 1999," November 22, 1999.

30   Division of STD Prevention, "Prevention of Genital HPV Infection and Sequelae: Report of an External Consultants' Meeting," 7.

31   Cf. Bearman, et al., "Chains of Affection: The Structure of Adolescent Romantic and Sexual Networks," *American Journal of Sociology* 110:1 (2004): 44-91.

32   Joe McIlhaney, M.D., *Safe Sex* (Grand Rapids, MI: Baker Book House, 1991), 23.

33   Cf. Medical Institute for Sexual Health, *Sex, Condoms, and STDs: What We Now Know* (Austin, TX: Medical Institute for Sexual Health, 2002); B. Dillion, "Primary HIV Infections Associated with Oral Transmission," CDC's 7th Conference on Retroviruses and Opportunistic Infections, Abstract 473, San Francisco, February 2000; Centers for Disease

Control, "Transmission of Primary and Secondary Syphilis by Oral Sex—Chicago, Illinois, 1998-2002," *Morbidity and Mortality Weekly Report* 51:41 (October 22, 2004): 966-968.

34 Cf. C. Sonnex, et al., "Detection of Human Papillomavirus DNA on the Fingers of Patients with Genital Warts," *Sexually Transmitted Infections* 75 (1999): 317–319; Winer, et al., "Genital Human Papillomavirus Infection: Incidence and Risk Factors in a Cohort of Female University Students," *American Journal of Epidemiology* 157:3 (2003): 218-226; Tabrizi, et al., "Prevalence of Gardnerella vaginalis and Atopobium vaginae in virginal women," *Sexually Transmitted Diseases* 33:11 (November 2006): 663-665.

35 Cf. Ley, et al., "Determinants of Genital Human Papillomavirus Infection in Young Women," *Journal of the National Cancer Institute* 83:14 (July 1991): 997-1003; Pao, et al., "Possible non-sexual transmission of genital human papillomavirus infections in young women," *European Journal of Clinical Microbiology & Infectious Diseases* 12:3 (March 1993): 221-223.

36 Cf. Hammarstedt, et al., "Human papillomavirus as a risk factor for the increase in incidence of tonsillar cancer," *International Journal of Cancer* 119:11 (December 2006): 2620-2623.

37 Centers for Disease Control, "Tracking the Hidden Epidemics, Trends in STDs in the United States 2000," (April 6, 2001), 6.

38 Cf. P. Leone, "Type-specific Serologic Testing for Herpes Simplex Virus-2," *Current Infectious Disease Reports* 5:2 (April 2003): 159-165.

39 Cf. Bosch, et al., "Male Sexual Behavior and Human Papillomavirus DNA: Key Risk Factors for Cervical Cancer in Spain," *Journal of the National Cancer Institute* 88:15 (August 1996): 1060-1067.

40 Haishan Fu, et al., "Contraceptive Failure Rates: New Estimates from the 1995 National Survey of Family Growth," *Family Planning Perspectives* 31:2 (March/April 1999): 61.

41 Santelli, et al., "Contraceptive Use and Pregnancy Risk Among U.S. High School Students, 1991–2003," *Perspectives on Sexual and Reproductive Health* 38:2 (June 2006): 109.

42 Cf. Yovel, et al., "The Effects of Sex, Menstrual Cycle, and Oral Contraceptives on the Number and Activity of Natural Killer Cells," *Gynecologic Oncology* 81:2 (May 2001): 254-262; Blum, et al., "Antisperm Antibodies in Young Oral Contraceptive Users," *Advances in Contraception* 5 (1989): 41–46; Critchlow, et al., "Determinants of cervical ectopia and of cervicitis: age, oral contraception, specific cervical infection, smoking, and douching," *American Journal of Obstetrics and Gynecology* 173:2 (August 1995): 534-43.

43 Cf. Baeten, et al., Hormonal contraception and risk of sexually transmitted disease acquisition: results from a prospective study," *American Journal of Obstetrics and Gynecology* 185:2 (August 2001): 380-385; Ley, et al., "Determinants of Genital Human Papillomavirus Infection in Young Women," *Journal of the National Cancer Institute* 83:14 (July 1991): 997–1003; Prakash, et al., "Oral contraceptive use induces upregulation of the CCR5 chemokine receptor on CD4(+) T cells in the cervical epithelium of healthy women," *Journal of Reproductive Immunology* 54 (March 2002): 117-131; Wang, et al., "Risk of HIV infection in oral contraceptive pill users: a meta-analysis," *Journal of Acquired Immune Deficiency Syndromes* 21:1 (May 1999): 51-58; Lavreys, et al., "Hormonal contraception

and risk of HIV-1 acquisition: results from a 10-year prospective study," *AIDS* 18:4 (March 2004): 695-697.

44 Cf. Chris Kahlenborn, MD, et al., "Oral Contraceptive Use as a Risk Factor for Premenopausal Breast Cancer: A Meta-analysis," *Mayo Clinic Proceedings* 81:10 (October 2006): 1290-1302; Collaborative Group on Hormonal Factors in Breast Cancer, "Breast cancer and hormonal contraceptives: collaborative reanalysis of individual data on 53,297 women with breast cancer and 100,239 women without breast cancer from 54 epidemiological studies," *Lancet* 347 (June 1996): 1713-1727; World Health Organization, "IARC Monographs Programme Finds Combined Estrogen-Progestogen Contraceptives and Menopausal Therapy are Carcinogenic to Humans," International Agency for Research on Cancer, Press Release 167 (July 29, 2005).

45 Cf. Smith, et al., "Cervical cancer and use of hormonal contraceptives: A systematic review," *Lancet* 361 (2003): 1159–1167.

46 Cf. World Health Organization, "IARC Monographs Programme Finds Combined Estrogen-Progestogen Contraceptives and Menopausal Therapy are Carcinogenic to Humans," International Agency for Research on Cancer, Press Release 167 (July 29, 2005); La Vecchia, "Oral contraceptives and cancer," *Minerva Ginecologica* 58:3 (June 2006): 209-214.

47 Cf. *Physicians' Desk Reference*, 2415; Kemmeren, et al., "Third generation oral contraceptives and risk of venous thrombosis: meta analysis," *British Medical Journal* 323 (July 2001): 131–134; Parkin, et al., "Oral contraceptives and fatal pulmonary embolism," *The Lancet* 355:9221 (June 2000): 2133-2134; Hedenmalm, et al., "Fatal venous thromboembolism associated with different combined oral contraceptives," *Drug Safety* 28:10 (2005): 907-916; Sameuelsson, et al., "Mortality from venous thromboembolism in young Swedish women and its relation to pregnancy and use of oral contraceptives," *European Journal of Epidemiology* 20:6 (2005): 509-516.

48 Cf. *Physicians' Desk Reference*, 2409, 2620-2621; Morrison, et al., "Hormonal Contraceptive Use, Cervical Ectopy, and the Acquisition of Cervical Infections," *Sexually Transmitted Diseases* 31:9 (September 2004): 561–567; U.S. Food and Drug Administration, "Ortho Evra (norelgestromin/ethinyl estradiol) Information," Department of Health and Human Services (September 20, 2006).

49 Johnson and Johnson, SEC Filing, Quarterly Report for Period Ending 10/1/2006; Associated Press, "Birth control patch linked to higher fatality rate," July 20, 2005.

50 http://www.ctv.ca/CTVNews/TopStories/20051219/depo_provera_051219/, "Class action suit filed over birth control drug," (December 19, 2005).

51 U.S. Food and Drug Administration, "Black Box Warning Added Concerning Long-Term Use of Depo-Provera Contraceptive Injection," FDA Talk Paper (November 17, 2004).

52 "The Case Against Depo-Provera: Problems in the U.S.," *Multinational Monitor* 6:2-3 (February/March 1985); Depo-Provera, Patient Labeling, Pharmacia & Upjohn Company (October 2004).

53 Cf. T.A. Kiersch, "Treatment of sex offenders with Depo-Provera," *The Bulletin of the American Academy of Psychiatry and the Law* 18:2 (1990): 179-187; Assembly Bill 3339, "An

act to repeal and add Section 645 of the Penal Code, relating to crimes," California State Senate, Amended August 20, 1996; 2005; California Penal Code, 645.

54 Cf. *Physicians' Desk Reference*, 2414, 2626, 2411; Larimore, et al., "Postfertilization Effects of Oral Contraceptives and Their Relationship to Informed Consent," *Archives of Family Medicine* 9 (2000): 126-133.

55 Cf. *Physicians' Desk Reference*, 1068; Plan B* (Levonorgestrel) Prescribing Information, Duramed Pharmaceuticals, Inc. (August 2006); Pontifical Academy for Life, "Statement on the So-Called 'Morning-After Pill,'" Vatican City (October 31, 2000).

56 Cf. Fergusson, et al., "Abortion in young women and subsequent mental health," *Journal of Child Psychology and Psychiatry* 47:1 (January 2006): 16-24; Gissler, et al., "Suicides after pregnancy in Finland, 1987-94: register linkage study," *British Medical Journal* 313 (December 1996): 1431-1434.

57 Cf. Jeff Brand, *Marital Duration and Natural Family Planning* (Cincinnati, OH: Couple to Couple League).

58 Cloud and Townsend, *Boundaries in Dating* (MI.: Zondervan Publishing House, 2000), 251.

59 Ryan, et al., "The First Time: Characteristics of Teens' First Sexual Relationships," 2.

60 Cf. Hsu G., "Statutory Rape: The dirty secret behind teen sex numbers," *Family Policy* (1996): 1-16.

61 Archbishop Fulton J. Sheen, as quoted in *True Girl* 1:1 (February/March 2006).

62 Cf. Karol Wojtyła, *The Way to Christ*

63 Foundation for the Family, *Practicing Teen Chastity*, Cincinnati, OH.

64 John Paul II, general audience of October 8, 1980.

65 John Paul II, general audience of June 27, 1984.

66 Pier Giorgio Frassati, "To the Catholic Youth of Pollone," 1923.

67 Cf. Karol Wojtyła, *Love and Responsibility*, 208.

Printed in the USA
CPSIA information can be obtained
at www.ICGtesting.com
CBHW031204200823
1006CB00001B/1